I Wish, I Wish

PAUL SHIPTON

Illustrated by John Eastwood

PACIFIC
LEARNING

This Americanized Edition of *I Wish, I Wish*,
originally published in English in 1996, is published
by arrangement with Oxford University Press.

05 04 03 02 01
10 9 8 7 6 5 4 3 2 1

Published by
Pacific Learning
P.O. Box 2723
Huntington Beach, CA 92647-0723
www.pacificlearning.com

ISBN: 1-59055-040-4
PL-7408

Contents

1

Something for Nothing

Kayla counted out the money for the tenth time. It didn't add up to much, even with the money from her old piggy bank and the change she had found in the seat cushions of the couch. Two dollars and thirty-four cents, to be exact.

"You should watch how you spend your money," said her sister, Vicky.

Vicky was full of practical advice, and Kayla always found it worthless.

"You could get a paper route – like the one I have," said Vicky, "and then you could put your money in a savings account – like I do."

Kayla liked the idea of having money, but she didn't like the idea of earning it. Getting out of her cozy bed on rainy and windy mornings? No thanks!

She said, "There isn't *time* for me to get a job before Mom's birthday. I'll never get her a good present with *this* much money."

Oh, I don't know. You have enough to buy one glove...

Ha, ha. Very funny.

Vicky shrugged. "You can't get something for nothing," she said.

Kayla sighed. Her sister was right. She'd never be able to afford a nice present. Then she had an idea. There was a secondhand store on Maple Street. She would be able to find a present there, even if it wasn't brand new. *Anyway,* she told herself, *it's the thought that counts.*

Twenty minutes and a speedy bike ride later, Kayla was standing inside the secondhand shop.

It was crowded and gloomy, and it was packed full of all kinds of things – old tables and chairs, rusty bike frames, and old photos. Some of the stuff looked okay, but most of it… well, *junk* was the word that popped into Kayla's head.

Plus, there were no price tags on anything. Kayla had no idea which things she could afford. The man behind the counter didn't rush over to help – he sat there, as still as a statue, reading his newspaper.

Kayla was starting to think this hadn't been such a good idea after all... Then she saw it.

It was a small brass lamp. It was old and battered. *That's because it's an antique*, Kayla told herself, *and Mom loves antiques*. She picked it up carefully. It was perfect – or at least it *would* be perfect once it had been cleaned up. Did she have enough money to buy it?

How much is this?

The man's eyes flickered up from his paper for an instant.

"Two dollars and thirty-four cents," he said.

Kayla couldn't believe it – that was exactly how much money she had! It was a sign that this was the right present to buy.

2

Mr. Moneygrubber

Kayla put the lamp carefully into the basket on her bike. She didn't want to damage it more on the ride home.

She was about to set off when a big, fancy car pulled up outside the shop. No, make that a *huge,* fancy car.

A thin-faced man in a long coat stepped out. He was followed by a big man in a suit and mirror sunglasses (even though it wasn't sunny). *He must be a bodyguard,* thought Kayla.

The two men marched into the
secondhand store.

*I never knew people like that went to
secondhand stores*, thought Kayla
with a shrug. Then she hopped on her
bike and started pedaling home. She
couldn't wait to show Vicky the lamp.

She had only been riding for a few
minutes when she heard a honking
horn behind her. It was the same big
car. It passed her and then screeched
to a halt. Kayla barely managed to
stop in time.

The back window slid down slowly and the thin-faced man leaned out.

The man gave a thin-lipped smile. It didn't put Kayla's mind at ease.

"My apologies," he said. "Jenkins, my driver, is sometimes a little too... eager. Let me introduce myself – my name is Charles Moneygrubber."

His smile widened and Kayla saw all his teeth gleaming. It made her think of a crocodile.

Of course, she knew that she should not talk to strangers and she was about to put her helmet back on and ride away – fast.

Then Moneygrubber said:

"You must be wondering why we stopped you... Well, for many years I have been looking for... something. This morning I was told that I might find it in a secondhand store. I got there as quickly as I could, but I found that it has just been sold... to you."

So that was it – the lamp! This Moneygrubber guy wanted the lamp!

Kayla shrugged. "Oh well, better luck next time."

Moneygrubber's eyes were cold.
"I'm afraid you do not understand.
The lamp is not valuable in terms of
money, but it has great *sentimental*
value to me. I want that lamp and I
am willing to buy it from you."

Kayla gasped. Had
she heard right? Two hundred dollars!
It was incredible.

She took the lamp out of the basket, ready to hand it over. Then she saw a twinkle of greed in Moneygrubber's eyes and a new thought jumped into her mind: *Hold on! Maybe it's worth MORE than two hundred dollars – in fact, maybe it's worth much more!*

She shook her head.

I don't think so.

Fine! I'll give you $1,000 for it.

Moneygrubber's voice got louder and there were two little, angry red spots on his pale cheeks.

Kayla didn't know what to say. A thousand dollars was a lot of money, but maybe this lamp was worth even more. Maybe it was a priceless antique. There was definitely something about Mr. Moneygrubber that Kayla didn't trust.

She shook her head one more time and the smile on Moneygrubber's face vanished. He stared at her with cold eyes and shouted to the other man inside the car.

The big man in the sunglasses leaped out of the car and rushed toward her.

He was fast, but Kayla was hard to beat on a bicycle. She tossed the lamp back into the basket and took off pedaling down the road. She heard the big man huff and puff as he tried to keep up with her on foot.

Then she heard the car roar into life again. It wouldn't take long to catch up with her. Luckily there was a bike path ahead – no car could follow her along that. If she could only make it there...

She forced her legs to go faster. Behind her the roar of the engine was getting louder. The big car was getting closer and closer...

Just before the car caught up with her, Kayla swerved over to the bike path. She was safe! Behind her she could hear the angry blare of the car's horn and a howl of rage from inside the car.

She rode home as fast as she could.

3

The Secret of the Lamp

Kayla couldn't wait to tell Vicky all about the lamp, but her older sister was studying at a friend's house. There would be no one home for fifteen minutes, according to Vicky's note.

She carefully put the lamp on the kitchen table. It didn't look very special, but Kayla knew it had to be worth a lot. Why else was that creepy Mr. Moneygrubber so desperate to get his hands on it?

Slowly Kayla made a plan. She would give the lamp as a birthday present to her mom.

Then they could take it to an antique dealer to find out what it was worth. Then… She began to imagine how they could spend all of that money.

First of all she decided to polish it. She grabbed a rag and began to rub the lamp.

There was a sound like thunder and then a flash of light. The kitchen filled with smoke, and there was a smell like old socks and rotten bananas.

As soon as the smoke cleared, Kayla saw with a shock that she was not alone anymore. A strange-looking man was standing in the kitchen.

He wore a suit and tie. (That wasn't so strange.)

His hair was combed and he carried a briefcase. (That wasn't very strange either.)

He was bright green, and he was so tall his head almost bumped the ceiling. (Now *that* was strange.)

Kayla was too stunned to speak. She opened and closed her mouth, but no sound came out.

Kayla was not the kind of person to stay stunned for long.

"What did you expect?" said the genie. "Isn't this the twenty-first century? A genie can follow fashion too, you know. Oh, I guess you're right – maybe this is a *little* formal."

He clicked his fingers – SNAP! – and he was wearing a T-shirt and jeans.

The genie shook his head impatiently.

"Not anymore. The Genies' Union voted to get rid of that system... oh, two hundred years ago. It wasn't working out. We weren't happy in our jobs, and the wishers weren't satisfied with the service, so we started a new system for wishes."

Which is?

The owner of the lamp can make any wish within two hours. After that, I return to the lamp.

Now, if I can just explain the other rules...

Kayla's mind was racing. Just think of all the things she could get… but the clock was ticking! Only two hours!

She said quickly, "That's okay, don't worry about the details. Now did you say 'any wish'? So, for example, if I say I want a million dollars…"

"Very well," sighed the genie, sounding rather bored. He clicked his fingers and… nothing happened.

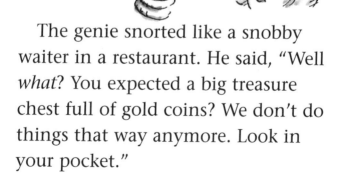

The genie snorted like a snobby waiter in a restaurant. He said, "Well *what*? You expected a big treasure chest full of gold coins? We don't do things that way anymore. Look in your pocket."

Kayla pulled out a piece of paper. It was a bank statement and it was in her name.

"It says one million dollars and twenty-four cents," she read out loud.

"The twenty-four cents was already in your account," explained the genie coolly.

Kayla grinned and rubbed her hands together. It was time to get down to business...

4

A Surprise for Vicky

When Vicky came home from
studying, at first she thought she was
going crazy. The street looked the
same as always, except for their little
house... It was gone! In its place stood
a huge palace. It had a row of white
pillars at the front, and two stone
lions guarded the front door.

In a daze, Vicky went up the walk.
The yard, which used to have a
birdbath and an old tire swing, now
looked like the grounds of a palace.

The hedges were trimmed into perfect animal shapes. A herd of white horses grazed in the meadows beyond.

Inside the house, it was even more amazing. The floors were made from the finest marble and beautiful paintings hung on every wall. There was gold everywhere, and the hallway led to the biggest double staircase she had ever seen.

In the kitchen Vicky found Kenny Baron – Kayla's very favorite rock star – eating caviar out of a salad bowl.

Hey! You're just in time! I was about to play some more tunes. Do want an autograph?

Vicky wandered open-mouthed through what had once been the dining room. It was an indoor Olympic-size swimming pool now.

At last she found Kayla in the huge living room.

Seeing that giant green face was the last straw for Vicky. She fainted.

When she woke up again, the same green face was looming over her. It hadn't been a bad dream. Her sister was beaming at her.

What's going on?

Promise you won't faint again?

Vicky nodded, and Kayla began to explain all about the genie and the lamp.

There's one thing I don't understand. Why don't the neighbors think it's weird that we're suddenly millionaires living in a palace?

Kayla just tapped her head and winked slyly.

I already thought of that, Vick. I wished that no one around here would notice any of the changes.

Vicky gulped. She was just beginning to realize that it was all real.

So what else did you wish for?

Oh, the usual things. Incredible riches, success, and good health... all that stuff. Mom and Dad are going to be so surprised!

Vicky was too shocked to reply.

I guess you were wrong, Vick. Sometimes you CAN get something for nothing. All these wishes cost nothing!

She grinned and waved at all the amazing things around them.

That's when things began to go very wrong...

5

Deep Trouble

The genie leaned forward and gave a polite cough.

Ahem. I couldn't help overhearing... but did you say "nothing"?

Kayla got a bad feeling deep in the pit of her stomach. This didn't sound like good news. She nodded.

I'm afraid that's not true. I was trying to explain everything to you earlier – but you didn't let me finish. The Genies' Union has changed the rules of wishing.

Yes, I know. I wish for two hours, then you go back into the lamp.

The genie raised one eyebrow.

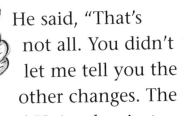

He said, "That's not all. You didn't let me tell you the other changes. The Genies' Union has just decided that we should be paid for what we do. Why should we go around granting wishes for free? So at the end of each two-hour period, the wisher is now given a bill."

The truth hit Kayla hard, like a speeding train.

A bill? You mean I have to pay for all this?

"Of course," said the genie smoothly. "Palaces aren't cheap, you know – not to mention all the other stuff. That rock singer in the kitchen was very expensive – overpriced, if you ask me."

Vicky shook her head. Her little sister was in deep trouble.

So where's the bill?

The genie clicked his fingers, and a long bill appeared in the air – a *very* long bill.

Kayla felt as if she couldn't breathe. A desperate idea leaped into her mind.

"It won't work," said Vicky. "You'd have to pay for the money you wished for on top of all the other stuff."

"Plus interest," added the genie.

Panic tightened its grip on Kayla. Was there no way out?

The genie looked businesslike. "There is another way, of course, to pay the bill. You can work it off in one of the factories where we have all the wish items built."

He glanced again at the bill and pulled out a calculator from thin air.

"That's impossible!" gasped Vicky, but Kayla just shook her head sadly.

The genie gave his "snobby waiter" snort again.

Kayla looked sadly at her solid-gold, diamond-studded watch. Only forty minutes before the two hours were up. What could she do?

Then Vicky spoke up.

For the first time she sounded like her usual bossy self again.

6

Against the Rules

Time was running out, but Vicky skimmed through the copy of the rules as quickly as she could. The print was tiny, and she had to squint and hold her head right next to the paper to read it.

At first it looked hopeless. There didn't seem to be any way out. The wisher was not allowed to wish that the past two hours had never happened, or anything like that. But then...

"If the owner sells the lamp to another person (not including the person from whom she or he bought the lamp) within the two hours, then the wishes made shall become null and void, and the contract terminated."

Kayla scratched her head.

43

"Don't you get it?"
cried Vicky. "If you sell
the lamp before the two
hours are up, then all of
the wishes will disappear
and you won't have to
pay. You can't sell it
back to the store, though,
and you've only got... twenty
minutes! The only thing is, who could
you sell it to?"

It hit Kayla in a flash.

Moneygrubber!
Moneygrubber knows
about the lamp – but he
doesn't know
EVERYTHING about it.

Kayla told her sister how
Moneygrubber had tried to take the
lamp from her.

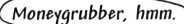

Moneygrubber, hmm.

Kayla turned to the genie.

Genie, can you take me to Charles Moneygrubber?

The genie shook his head stiffly. "It's against the rules, I'm afraid. Clause 91, Section C. *'No wishes may be used to find a new buyer.'* I cannot do *a single thing* to help you find a new buyer."

"There's no need!" cried Vicky. "I've seen that name before. I've seen it on a gate, on my paper route. It's that big house up on Thistle Hill."

45

Kayla jumped up.

He seemed to shimmer and turn to smoke. Then he shot up the spout and into the lamp.

She scooped up the lamp and charged outside to her bike.

7

A Race against Time

Kayla rode like never before. She pushed down on the pedals with all her might. The genie's lamp rattled in her basket. On she rode.

Fifteen minutes to go... don't stop now! she thought to herself.

She made a sharp left and felt the wind hit her head on. She gritted her teeth and forced her legs to push harder, to go faster. She zoomed down hills and she puffed and panted up hills. On she rode.

Ten minutes to go... keep going...
nine minutes...

A dog jumped out at her, barking crazily. She nearly fell off her bike, but she managed to keep her balance and keep going. On she rode.

Eight minutes until the time was up...
would she make it?

Kayla was now on the road that led to Moneygrubber's house. Her legs ached, but she never slowed down. Her heart pounded, *baDUM, baDUM, baDUM.* The pedals flew under her.

Five minutes...

At last she reached the driveway! She zoomed up the gravel path and leaped off her bike. She rang the doorbell...

and waited...

 ... and waited.

No answer.
Was anyone home? Would anyone ever come to the door?
Two minutes to go...

The door opened a crack and Moneygrubber's thin face peered out at her.

When he saw Kayla with the lamp, his eyes gleamed like a hungry tiger.

"I've changed my mind!" gasped Kayla. "You can have the lamp!"

Moneygrubber was greedy, but he was no fool. His cold eyes narrowed in suspicion.

He said, "*Why* have you changed your mind? Furthermore, how did you find me?"

Kayla's mind raced frantically. She pointed at the giant car that was parked in the driveway.

She gasped, "I knew you lived here because I saw the car. I want to sell the lamp because I didn't realize it was in such bad condition. Look, it's got a big dent on one side."

She held the lamp up for him to see and thought to herself, *PLEASE BELIEVE ME! I'M ALMOST OUT OF TIME!*

"So you noticed nothing unusual about the lamp?" asked Moneygrubber sharply.

Kayla shook her head. She pretended not to see the sparkle of greed in his eye.

Kayla did not hesitate.

Moneygrubber dug a bony hand
into his pocket and tossed a ten-dollar
bill to her. Then he snatched the lamp
and slammed the door shut.

Kayla looked down at the money
in her hand – ten whole dollars.
She grinned.

8

After It All

The next day Kayla and Vicky
were walking home from school.
Everything was back to normal. All
the things Kayla had wished for were
gone. The genie had done his work
well, and no one remembered that
anything unusual had ever happened.
The genie had even made *Vicky* forget
all about it.

Only Kayla knew the truth.

So what are you going to
get Mom for her
birthday?

"I don't know," said Kayla. "I've got ten dollars I wasn't expecting. Maybe I'll get a craft book out of the library and make her something. After all, it's the thought that counts."

They came to a newsstand.

"Oh, hey, I meant to tell you – they need another person for the paper route. Are you interested?"

For a moment, Kayla almost said "yes." *Almost.* Then she thought of how nice it was to be warm in bed in the morning, and how lousy it must be to trudge through the wind and rain carrying a big load of newspapers.

We'll see...

About the Author

When I was growing up,
I always wanted to be an
astronaut, a professional
soccer player, or (if those
didn't work out for any
reason) maybe a rock star.
So it came as something
of a shock when I became
first a teacher and then an editor of
educational books.

I have lived in England and Turkey. I'm
still on the run and now live in Chicago,
Illinois, with my wife and family.

I know a girl like Kayla, and the
girl in this story is based on her!

Paul Shipton